About this Book

Do you live near a canal? Many people do, without knowing it. Some canals have now dried up and others look like ordinary rivers. In cities they are often hidden away behind tall buildings. Yet once everyone knew where the canals were because they waited eagerly for barges to come bringing them coal, tea and sugar. Everyone has these things today, but before the canals were built in the eighteenth century most people had to go without them because they were so expensive.

This book shows how the canals served cities like Birmingham, Manchester and Liverpool and what life was like for the canal folk—the boatmen, lock keepers, dockers and navvies. It shows, too, how the railways came and seized trade from the canals, many of which fell into disuse. The great days of canal building only lasted about forty years, but it was an exciting time. The pictures in this new Eyewitness title help you to understand that excitement and to see why many people today are interested in re-opening the canals—just for fun.

Some of the words printed in *italics* may be new to you. You can look them up in the word list on page 92.

AN EYEWITNESS BOOK

Canals

JANE DORNER

WAYLAND PUBLISHERS LONDON

More Eyewitness Books

Frontispiece: Barton Bridge in 1793

Contents

The Beginnings

There were no canals in England before the 18th century. Cargo carrying vessels used the rivers where possible but of course rivers did not go everywhere. So packhorses, or waggons, carried goods like coal, sugar and tea to the small towns and villages. As horses could not carry much, these items were very expensive and only the rich could afford them.

Journeys were slow because roads were dangerous. An eyewitness said travellers "will meet with ruts which I actually measured 4 feet deep and floating with mud . . ." Waggons often overturned. So people looked towards other forms of transport.

The 18th century was a time of invention. Factories in the north were producing new machines and original processes. They needed to get hold of raw materials quickly and cheaply. The canals made this possible. At first only the areas round Manchester and Liverpool benefitted, but as more canals were built, transport became better.

However there were a lot of people who did not want more canals. Farmers were afraid they would cut across their fields. Millers were worried that water would be drained away from their rivers. Some groups just did not want canals because they thought they would spoil the scenery. But Parliament approved the first canal plan and from then on there was no holding back.

THE RIVER. London's River Thames was used for many years as the city's main highway. There was only one bridge and the easiest way of getting from place to place was by boat. The picture shows how busy the river was. It was painted on a festival day, but there was a lot of traffic on ordinary days too. How many boats can you see?

RAFTS. When people wanted to transport goods along a river, they often used rafts. The man in the picture above is using a pole to bring his raft near to the shore. It is made of logs of wood tied firmly together. As it is flat, the man can roll his cargo onto it and then float down river.

WEIRS. One difficulty with river travel is that in some places the current is fast and in others it is slow, and the depth of the water varies. *Weirs* were built to control the current. This made *navigation* easier. The only trouble was that millers worked the weirs because they needed the water power to grind their corn. The mill wheel in the picture makes the power. Vessels wanting to pass might have to wait days until the miller was willing to let the water down into the lower stretch of river.

THE FERRY. Those who travelled by road had to use rivers too, because there were not many bridges. The bridge over the Thames in this picture is unfinished. So a ferry is taking the horse and cart to the other side. A long chain is stretched from one bank to the other: it passes through loops on the large floating platform. Strong men pull the chain through the loops so that the ferry moves.

ROAD TRANSPORT. Road travellers used large covered waggons, like the one in the picture, to transport their goods. This meant they had to have a lot of horses and it made the journey very expensive. If one horse tripped on a loose stone in the road, he might upset the whole waggon. The traveller would have to waste a lot of time putting everything to rights and mending anything that got broken. So his journey was very slow.

TURNPIKES. Another expense of road travel was the turnpike. Even though the roads were bad, those who used them had to pay a *toll*. This would amount to a lot of money on a long journey. You can see toll gates in the picture. On the side of the hut is a list of *tariffs*. The waggon which has just passed through the gates probably paid less than the stage coach which is approaching.

HIGHWAYMEN. One of the dangers of road travel was that there were a lot of highway robbers. The traveller in the picture looks like a farmer who is taking his produce from one village to another. He is probably not very rich, but the highwayman is threatening him with his life if he does not hand over money or his goods.

SANKEY BROOK. The first canal built in England was a stretch of water joining together two parts of the Sankey Brook on the River Mersey. The river twisted and turned so much that the straight canal made a short cut and river navigation was easier and quicker. Factories like the one in the picture were built on the river, because the owner knew he could transport his goods safely.

COAL. The factory in the previous picture, like many others, needed coal to fire its furnaces. Coal was probably the most important *commodity* in England during the 18th and 19th centuries, because of the growth of industry. Compare the two pictures on these pages and you will see why water transport was so much easier for heavy goods. In the top picture three men are labouring hard to fill one small cart with coal. By the time it gets to its destination the price of it will be very high.

In the bottom picture two boats are *moored* on a river right next to the *colliery*. Small trucks are carrying the coal from the mine shaft to the boats. It is tipped down a ramp onto the deck. The horse will

then pull the boat along the river. Because a boat is easier to pull, this horse can pull goods weighing sixty times as much as the carthorse.

MANCHESTER. Here are two pictures of an industrial city in the 18th century. You can see that Manchester was a gloomy place. There were lots of industries and they all relied on coal. If coal could be brought by water all the way into the city, then everyone would benefit.

THE BRIDGEWATER CANAL. It was the Duke of Bridgewater who built a canal to take coal into Manchester. He had mines at Worsley, $4\frac{1}{2}$ miles away. He thought up a scheme for the canal and, after overcoming several problems, he managed to get it built. Here he stands pointing with pride at the teams of men at work. You can see the canal and the river in the background. The canal is on an *aqueduct* crossing the river.

WORSLEY.   Two cranes are at work near the Duke's coal mines at Worsley. They are lowering sacks of coal onto the barges. The boats are then pulled up the canal. On the right you can see a *packet boat*. The Duke realised that canals could be used for people as well as transporting goods.

OPPOSITION. Not everyone liked the new canal. Look at the picture of the farmyard and you will see why. It is a busy scene and the farmer does not want his work disturbed by a canal cutting through part of his land. Canal builders often had to wait until they found farmers who were willing to sell stretches of land before they could plan routes.

The Builders

Nowadays when a new road is built, the government decides where it should go and how wide it should be. It is built from money out of our taxes. But in the 18th century private companies built both roads and canals. They charged a toll to allow people to use them, so that they could make a profit. How were canals built?

The company first elected a committee to deal with everyday matters. They had to appoint an engineer who designed the workings of the new canal. Then they put a bill through parliament to get approval for the scheme. Once this was done they negotiated with farmers to buy the land they needed for the canal. And, most important of all, they had to raise money for building materials and to pay the men who worked on the site.

The building works usually began at what were to be the two ends of the canal at once. Eventually the teams of workmen met in the middle, but this took many years. A tourist of the time wrote this about the construction works on the Bridgewater Canal: "I surveyed the Duke's men for two hours, and think the industry of bees, or labour of ants, is not to be compared with them. Each man's work seemed to depend, and be connected with his neighbour's . . ."

This chapter shows some of the problems the canal builders faced.

THE COMMITTEE. When a new canal was planned, a committee was elected by the men who put up the money for the project. Here is one committee puzzling over a proposed route. Some of them are arguing about it, but others are falling asleep over a report. What sort of decisions do you think this committee is making?

THE ROUTE. The course of a canal was hardly ever a straight line. Sometimes it had to go round a hill. Sometimes it had to make a *detour* because the local landowner objected to it. But it was a lot straighter than most rivers as you can see in the picture. The thick black line is the canal. Notice how many streams and rivers the canal crosses.

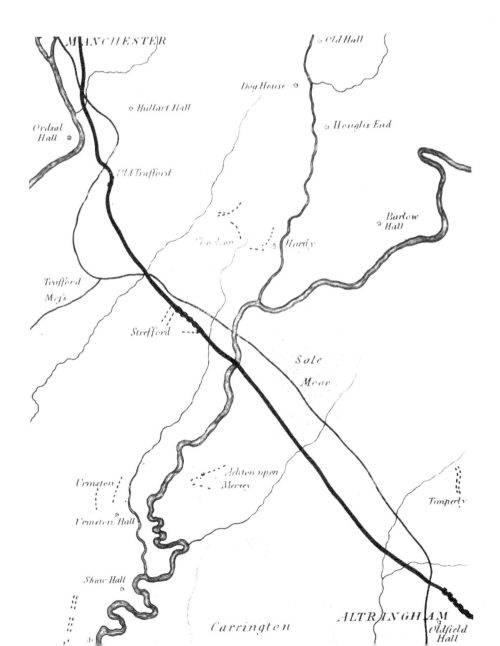

THE ENGINEERS. Two of the most important British canal engineers were James Brindley (left) and Thomas Telford (right). They would fix routes, control water flow and decide how to keep their canals level. There were hundreds of things that could go wrong and the engineer had to solve them all. Brindley used to go to bed and lie in the dark until he had thought it all out. He had no education and could not even read or write, but this did not stop him from being a very good engineer!

LEVELLING. What were the engineers problems? One of them was that water does not flow uphill. So he had to think out ways of pulling a load uphill. The pictures show one way in which this could be done. Can you see how it works? The only trouble about this method was that it could only pull small loads, so the cargo had to be loaded bit by bit onto barges.

LOCKS. A better solution was to use locks. Each lock has 2 sets of gates—the second set is just out of our picture. A boat comes in at the lower level and the gates close behind it. Then the first gates are opened and the water flows slowly into the lock, until it is level with the upper canal. This has happened on the right side of the above picture and the barges are ready to move on. Going downhill, the same thing happens in reverse.

INCLINED PLANES. The picture on the right shows another way in which boats could be pulled uphill or downhill. Here the boats are standing on a moving railed track which is rather like an escalator. In the pictures on page 27 the tubs had chains attached to the tops. The rail line is moved by water power.

A STAIRCASE.   If there was a very steep change in water level, the engineer built a staircase of locks, like the one in the picture above. Can you see how it works? Each lock lowered, or brought up the level of water, by about 8 feet. Can you work out how steep this slope is?

TUNNELS.   It was cheaper to go round hills even though this made the canal longer. If this was not possible the engineer built a tunnel. This was very hard work. The rock could be *blasted out* with .gunpowder, but most of the labour was done by men with picks and shovels. The Harecastle tunnel in the picture opposite took 11 years to build.

AQUEDUCTS. On page 25 you saw that a canal often had to cross several rivers, and so aqueducts were built. Workmen had to drive huge columns deep into the river bed. The canal was very heavy so the structure had to be quite firm. Teams of men kept up the work night and day so that the river would not destroy their work. On one aqueduct there were "127 labourers, 22 carpenters and 14 sawyers" at work.

BRIDGES. The canal company usually had to agree to build three to four bridges every mile so that people or farm animals could get across. Some of them were just planks of wood which could swing aside. When a bridge carried a road, it had to be solidly built. The bridge in the picture is in London. You can tell by the costumes of the people on this bridge that it is in a fashionable part of the city.

SKILLED WORKMEN. This brickmaker would be one of the skilled men working on the construction site. He had a lot to do as thousands of bricks were used to line the banks of the canal. Can you see how he is shaping the clay and pressing it into a mould? The bricks on the wheelbarrow are drying out. Other skilled workers were masons, carpenters, miners and blacksmiths.

NAVVIES.   The unskilled labourers who worked on the building were called "canal navigators" or "navvies" for short. Their main job was to make a cutting for the canal. They spent all day digging up the earth and then moving it in a wheelbarrow to make a bank further along the route. Others made the cutting waterproof by stamping a mixture of clay and water into the canal bed. This was called puddling You can imagine how tiring it was!

WATER. One of the engineer's greatest problems was finding water for the canal. If he pumped too much away from nearby rivers, the farmers and millers would complain. So he built reservoirs to catch rainwater. There are many water containers like these all along the canals. Some of them look like lakes. Can you guess how deep the water in a canal is? The picture on page 32 gives some idea.

THE MEN. The navvies had to be very tough men for the work was dirty and dangerous. Most of them drank a great deal and the villagers thought they were very rough. One man wrote "possessed of all the daring recklessness of the smuggler, without any of his redeeming qualities, their ferocious behaviour can only be equalled by the brutality of their language."

ACCOMMODATION. A committee member wrote: "the accommodation and markets near the intended canal . . . are so little adequate to the wants of a numerous body of workmen and labourers, that we have found it necessary to continue our attention to their habitation and subsistence." Usually the company only provided poor huts like the one in the picture. picture.

Canterbury Navigation & Sandwich Harbour.

THIS IS TO CERTIFY.

That The Mayor Jurats and Commonalty of the Town and Port of Sandwich are Subscribers for **One Share** of Twenty five Pounds in the Canterbury Navigation and Sandwich Harbour Company distinguished in the Books of the said Company by the Number *1211* dated the 31st day of October 1825.

Entered folio

Garrett & Nutt Clerks

All Transfers of Shares must be registered at the Office.

SHARES. The money for building the canal had to come from somewhere. So the company advertised asking people to buy shares in the new project. They gave a sum of money and in return they were allowed a share of the profits. The man who has bought this share has paid £25 for it. This was a great deal of money in those days. The navvies were then earning about 18p a day.

SPECULATORS.   Many of the men who bought the shares were already well off and were greedy for more money. Here they are riding hard to a purchasers' meeting. They are racing each other to get there first so that they will be sure of getting a share. They hoped to make considerable profits.

SEALS.   These are seals that the companies used for all their paperwork. The one of Chester shows a walled city because it is one of the two medieval cities which still has its walls. Which is the other? Can you see the Potteries in one of the other seals?

OPENING. When a canal opened there was a celebration. Everyone who had anything to do with the canal took part. An eyewitness described how one celebration began. The company "embarked on one of the barges which was handsomely decorated with flags. At the moment of this barge's moving forward an excellent band played *God Save the King,* and a salute of 21 guns was fired."

CANAL BASIN. This picture shows how busy life on the canals was. It is a meeting place of several canals at Stourport. Boats met here and transferred their cargo to barges travelling on a different canal. If you look at the picture closely, you can see men rolling barrels and horses pulling carts. Warehouses store goods overnight while they are waiting to be transferred to another boat.

Life on the Canals

Imagine a canal has now been opened. The celebrations are over and people want to get down to the serious business of using the canal. After all it was built for transport.

Horsedrawn tramcars pull the goods from the factory to the canal and the heavy work of loading begins. Iron, coal, metals, lime and timber are the commodities most often sent by canal. They are packed tightly into long boats and then covered with a *tarpaulin* so that they do not get too wet.

One of the best known carrying firms was called Pickfords. You saw one of their barges on page 33. They employed the bargemen who worked on the canals. Here is one of their advertisements: "Messrs Pickford's Fly Boats continue to load daily for London and *intermediate* places, as usual, and every attention is paid in forwarding and delivering Goods with the greatest Regularity and *Dispatch*. Rates of Freight &c., may be had by applying to their Agent . . ."

Canals were most popular in the 18th and early 19th centuries because no other form of transport was so cheap. All manufacturers wanted to send their goods across country by boat. Barges often had to queue up to use the locks or pass the tollhouses.

Who were the people who lived and worked on the canals? This chapter introduces you to some of them.

TOW HORSES. Men are very strong but one horse can pull a heavier load than 2 or 3 men. In the picture a horse is pulling along a well *laden* barge. Someone had to walk with the horse to lead him. Another man is sitting in the *stern* to steer the boat. A third man is ready with his pole in case he has to push the boat out of a muddy patch.

BOW HAULIERS. The *bargee* sometimes hired 2 or 3 men to pull his boat along the canal. In the picture on the right the men are pulling a rope which is attached to the tow mast. This mast could also be used for a sail on windy days. Bow hauliers got their name because they hauled along the *bow* of the boat. The rope they pull was normally fixed to the bow.

STEAM POWER. Another way of pulling boats along was by steam tug. The picture shows the first steam tug, *Charlotte Dundas*, towing on the Forth and Clyde Canal in 1802. The tug could pull several barges along at once but it was very expensive to hire and most canal men stuck to horses. The inset shows a section through the engine. The big water wheel drives the boat.

TOLL. The horses usually belonged to the bargee but not always. He could hire them from the canal company. This meant he could change his horses instead of waiting while the animals rested. It made the journey quicker. On the right you can see a toll ticket which the bargee would have used to show he had paid his money to hire horses. He also had to pay toll to travel on the canal.

STAMP OFFICE.

Nº 40

EXCHANGE TICKET.

KENT.

ecᵈ. a Ticket for   *Days*

from

HORSES 2.

THE CARGO. The Regent Canal runs into the Limehouse Docks on the River Thames. Barges came there to load their boats with wares which they took up north. Two of the boatmen opposite are using poles to *punt* with. This moves the boat along quite slowly.

WAREHOUSES. All canal companies had warehouses near the docks. Barges could not always be available to take goods straight off the ship. So they unloaded the cargo into a warehouse to be collected later by a bargee. Goods brought from the factories would also be stored until they could be collected. *The Ellen* in the picture below *plies* between London and Manchester.

BOAT BUILDING. When a barge came into the docks, it usually had a few days to spare before picking up the next load. This was a good time to do repairs. There were lots of boat builders near the docks who could lend a helping hand. The picture shows a building yard near Liverpool Docks. The wood comes to the yard as logs and then the men saw it into planks. In the sheds at the back of the picture you can see 3 barges under construction.

TRAFFIC CONTROL. Canal companies had their own boats which went up and down the waterway to make sure all was going well and to control the traffic. The Stroudwater Navigation Company in this picture has a rather fancy boat. There are even 3 hornplayers on board. Have you any idea why? Notice, too, the 3 bow hauliers labouring along the towpath.

PASSENGER BOATS. The canals were too exciting to be used only for cargo. Everyone wanted to travel in a boat, so the companies arranged short pleasure trips. The ladies and gentlemen in the picture above are enjoying the scenery on this summer's day. One man is looking into the distance with a telescope. These boats were also used for longer trips and passengers could book a *berth* below deck.

ROYAL PATRONAGE. Even Queen Victoria (1837–1901) wanted to travel on a canal. The picture opposite shows her barge on the Crinan Canal in Scotland. The four horses seem to be pulling it along at quite a speed. The canal companies were proud of the Queen's *patronage* because it encouraged other people to use the canals.

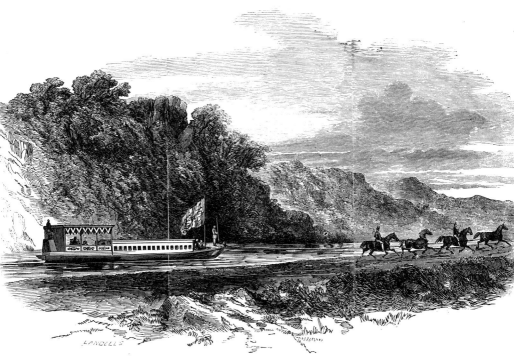

PASSAGE OF HER MAJESTY ON THE CRINAN CANAL.

LEGGERS. There were no towpaths through the tunnels because it was too expensive to build them. Look at the picture and you will see how the boat got through. Two men lay down on their backs on a plank at each side of the boat. They "walked" along the walls of the tunnel and the boat moved. They were called leggers and they waited at the entrance to be hired. It was a very dangerous job. If you fell off the plank into the pitch dark of the tunnel, you would probably drown.

THE LOCK KEEPER.   It is very easy to open a lock. Even this little girl can do it—with a bit of help from her father. He is the lock keeper and he keeps the key. The locks are fastened most of the time. This is because they use hundreds of gallons of water each time they are opened. Someone has to control the waterflow and make sure that not too much water is lost from one side of the canal.

DREDGING.   Every so often a canal company would send along a dredger to make sure there were no obstructions on the route. People often threw things into the water. The dredger fished them out again. A long chain is stretched to the floor of the canal. You can see the man in the bow winding it. If there is a big object in the canal he will feel it pull at the chain.

MOORING. Normally, a bargee's boat was his home, and that of his family, too. Here is a canal family which has tied up the boat for the evening. The horses are feeding and the crew is resting. They had to stop for the night because it got so dark they could not see. Anyway the locks and toll houses were closed, and a chain was put across the canal. Can you think why? The canal opened again one hour before sunrise.

THE CABIN. If you have ever been inside a caravan or the cabin of a boat, you will know just how little space there is. In the picture you can see a mattress rolled up out of the way. The bargee's wife has to keep the interior very tidy so that nothing gets lost. She has got some of the things she needs most often nailed to the wall so she knows where they are.

TEA TIME. In England we drink so much tea that we do not realize what a treat it was for a poor family in the 18th and early 19th centuries. This canal family can be glad because they have helped to make tea available to more people. Before the canals were built tea cost £10 a pound. The poor used to brew up the leaves that rich families threw away. Cheaper canal transport brought the price right down to a few shillings.

THE BOATMAN'S WIFE. It was a hard life being married to a boatman. Not only did the boatman's wife have to cook and to keep the cabin tidy, but she also had to help navigate. The woman in the picture is steering the boat along a difficult patch of the waterway.

CANAL CHILDREN. The children who were brought up on the canals suffered from their *nomadic* life. There was no room to play and be rowdy on board and the boat did not stop long at rest places. When the boat was moving they had to help because the bargee needed all hands to keep the boat moving. This poor girl is guiding the donkeys. She looks as if she is used to a life of hardship.

The Problems

Once there were 12,000 miles of canals threading their way across Britain. Now there are only 2,800 miles in use. How did this happen?

As private companies built the canals, no-one made sure that there was *uniformity* between them. Some were wide, others were very narrow and the depth of water varied. This meant that different kinds of boats were used on each type of canal. Some of them are shown on the next few pages. The trouble was that a boat carrying, say, a load of coal down one canal might not be able to travel along another which joined up with it. So the men would have to unload all their coal, carry it in carts to the other canal and reload onto a different boat. This slowed them down a great deal.

Then in the 19th century the steam engine was invented and everything changed. In 1830 the Liverpool and Manchester Railway opened. The Bridgewater Canal Company had to cut its rates to compete. Suddenly no-one wanted canal shares any longer. Now they rushed to put their money into the railways.

For a long time canals have been little used, but people are now interested in them again. The miles of waterway make attractive walks. Boating clubs are springing up and canal holidays in converted narrow boats are always fully booked up in the summer months.

SEVERN TROWS. The earliest canals used a flat bottomed boat, which had a square sail, like these two in the picture. There is no cabin and the men probably camped on land. You can see an awning supported by hoops on the stern of the boat in front. This was pulled over the cargo, and the men could shelter under it in wet weather. This type of boat was also called a frigate, keel or wherry.

THE BARGE. This was a boat built to navigate rivers. It was strong enough to cope with tidal changes, but could not go out to sea. River barges usually had a beam of over 14 feet, and this was too wide for most canals. The barge could be used, but two of them would not be able to pass.

NARROW BOAT. This was the boat most commonly used on the canals. They were nicknamed "starvationers" because they were so slim! They were usually about 74 feet long by 7 feet wide, though this varied a great deal. Some were even less wide where the locks on the canal were very narrow. This was because the engineer tried to save money by building the canal as narrow as possible. The trouble was that a boat from a wider canal could not use both.

PACKET BOATS. We saw a pleasure cruiser in the last chapter (page 54). The type of boat on the right was built to take travellers over long distances. They went at 2 to 4 m.p.h. This seems very slow but the passengers had a more comfortable journey than those who went by stage coach. These boats were wider than the narrow boats and they took priority over cargo-carrying vessels. These had to wait in a wider bit of the canal for the packet boat to pass.

MOTOR BOATS. This picture brings our brief
survey of canal boats right up to the 20th century. The
two small barges have now got motors and they can
chug along at a steady speed. This is the type of boat
now used for canal holidays. There are still a few in
use for cargo transport.

BREAKING UP OF THE ICE IN THE ST. LAWRENCE AT MONTREAL.

FREEZING. Many things slowed down canal transport. For instance, the canals would freeze up in the winter. The 3 men in the picture below are standing on the ice of the canal itself. There was nothing for it but to sit it out and wait for the canal to thaw. The top picture shows an icebreaker at work on the St. Lawrence Seaway in Canada. It is such a big machine that you can easily imagine why it could not be used on the canals.

ROADS. At the beginning of this book you read that roads in the 18th century were muddy dirt tracks. However this changed during the 19th century. Roads became smoother and there were better carriages. There was also a police system so the danger of highway robbers was not so great. Manufacturers started to send their goods by road again, so taking some trade away from the canals.

THE RAILWAYS. In the picture below a horse is plodding along the towpath pulling a narrow boat. Above a new railway train goes shooting past with its trucks of cargo. By the end of the 19th century railways were built almost all over Britain. Rail transport was much quicker and often cheaper as well. Many canals fell into disuse. The railway companies bought them up and converted them into railway tracks.

CANALS TODAY. Not many firms use canals for transport today. Big lorries have made it so much easier to send goods by road. But canals are still useful for carrying very heavy loads like timber, iron and steel. The picture shows a barge near the Potteries in the Midlands. Can you see the kilns? What might the barge be carrying in this area?

CANAL HOLIDAYS.   Lots of people enjoy holidays on the canals. Some just like cruising along and meeting other holiday makers at the mooring places. Others go because they like fishing. The canal companies look out for any pollution of the waters so that fishing can continue. Even the goat in the bottom picture is enjoying himself!

Ship Canals

Towards the end of the 19th century a number of far-seeing men realized that there was a place for larger modernized canals. Railways might take most of the ordinary *freight* across Britain, but a really big and efficient ship canal could increase trade with other countries. A Manchester engineer, called Daniel Adamson, was one of the pioneers of ship canals. He put up a plan to dig a wide cutting from Manchester all the way to the sea. Ships and freighters could then sail in and this would increase the town's trade. Building the Manchester Ship Canal was a major *feat* of engineering and involved many problems. It was finally opened in 1894 by Queen Victoria.

Other big ship canals are the Caledonian and Crinan in Scotland, the Bristol Channel Canal, the Dutch Nordzee Canal, the Kiel in Denmark and the Corinth in Greece. Most famous of all are the Suez Canal in the Middle East and the Panama in South America. The pictures on the following pages will show you some of these. As you read, find the canals in an atlas so that you know exactly where they are.

The new ship canals were very efficient. They have always made use of increased technical knowledge, and so they are developing all the time. Modern machinery such as cranes, lifts, *containers* and enormous lorries make the heavy work easier. The ship canals deal mainly with international trade.

HARBOUR WORKS. This is the harbour of the Nordzee canal in the Dutch town of Amsterdam. Huge ships carrying up to 2,000 tons of cargo load and unload here. You can see the workmen resting after moving the packing cases. They are too heavy to lift and the men have been using a rope and logs of wood to roll the cases along the pier.

THE CALEDONIAN. The canal on the right was built very early in the 19th century. Its purpose was to link the eastern and western seas so that ships would not have to sail right round the tip of Scotland. It joins together the locks of the Great Glen from Fort William to Inverness. You can see from the picture that the canal is very much wider than the small ones built for inland traffic.

SUEZ. The history of the Suez Canal is a sad one, because it has so often been closed for political reasons. It was built by a French company and it joins the Mediterranean to the Red Sea. The canal is a short-cut which saves ocean going vessels of all countries from going all the way round Africa. The map shows you the canal's route. At the north entrance is Port Said. You can see what this looked like in the early days in the picture on the right. The port at the southern end is Suez.

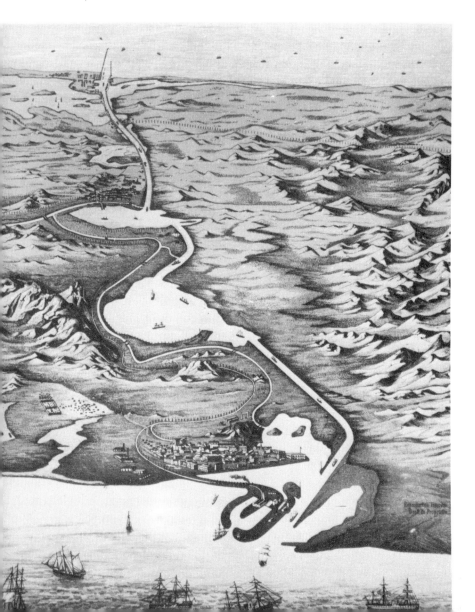

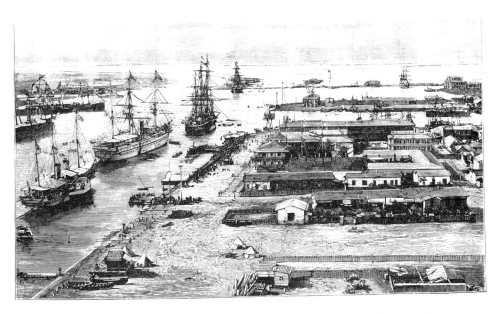

The canal goes 100 miles along a sandy desert. It was hot work building it and about 20,000 men were employed. They worked under Ferdinand de Lesseps, a Frenchman. Work was often slowed down by outbreaks of cholera. Finally, in 1869, the canal opened. It was not at first a great success and the shareholders lost a lot of money. In 1875 Disraeli, who was the British Prime Minister, managed to buy almost half the shares for only £4 million. Later these shares made Britain very rich.

PANAMA.   By 1881 de Lesseps was an old man, but he was hard at work planning a new canal. This cut through a narrow mountain range in South America at the *isthmus* of Panama. The canal is only 50 miles long and it links the Atlantic and Pacific oceans. At the beginning of the project the people were very optimistic and arranged this reception for de Lesseps. His portrait appears in the arch.

But everything went wrong. Fifty thousand workmen died from disease or overwork. One thousand
million French francs were spent and still the canal
was not finished. The picture shows what hard work
it was making a cutting through the mountains. In
the end there was a trial and de Lesseps was accused
of making a mess of the whole project. Later the
Americans took over and in 1914 the canal opened.

CANAL WORKS. This picture shows how far building techniques had improved when the Manchester Ship Canal was built. Compare this with the pictures on pages 34 and 35. There are still men with wheelbarrows but look at the big steam machines. They were called steam navvies and they could lift heavy weights. There is a railway track near by which brought heavy building materials right to the site.

THE CORINTH. One of the most spectacular canals is the straight Corinth, in the picture on the right. This links the Gulf of Corinth to the Aegean Sea. It is only 4 miles long and as you can see in this picture, runs through a deep cutting with towering rock sides. Do you think it would be exciting to be on board the ship?

MANCHESTER SHIP CANAL. Here is a modern picture of the great ship canal. This stretch goes under the Bridgewater Canal. If you look closely you can see narrow boats near the gas works. The thing that looks like a swing bridge that has opened to let the big ship through is really an aqueduct. It is carrying water and it joins the two sections of the Bridgewater Canal. The bridge has replaced the one that you can see on the frontispiece of this book.

MECHANIZATION. This is a steam powered dredger. Its job was to deepen and widen the ship canals. Compare it with the one on page 58. The ship canals did not have to be puddled like the inland cuttings, so this machine could be used to dig up earth when water was already in the canal. Underneath are buckets attached to chains. They pull up earth and mud.

CANAL LIFTS. The old canals had a staircase of locks when the change in land level was very great. It was a slow system. Now a lift can be used. The boat in the picture above is floated in a tub of water which is really a lift. It is slowly brought down to the lower level of the canal. Other boats on the right of the picture are waiting to use the lift as it can only take one boat at a time.

CONTAINERS. The two transporter cranes in the picture opposite are lowering containers into the hold of the liner. The goods are first packed into enormous boxes and these can be quickly transferred to the waiting ship. This one holds about 500 containers and it takes 48 hours to load. The smaller boat at the liner's side is a tug which will pull the ship out of harbour.

ROLL ON—ROLL OFF. At all big ports facilities are available to transport very heavy loads of about 300 tons. Things like electricity generating equipment can best be moved by being rolled onto the deck. The picture shows how this is done. Canals are ideal for this kind of work because transport of heavy loads is cheaper by water. It also keeps down slow traffic on the roads.

Table of Dates

1759   The first stretch of canal by the Sankey Brook is opened
1761   The Bridgewater Canal is completed
1777   The Trent and Mersey Canal is built
1820   George IV is crowned
1822   The Caledonian Canal is built by Thomas Telford
1825   The first railway from Stockton to Darlington is built
1830   The Liverpool and Manchester Railway is built. It is the first one to compete with the canals
1837   Queen Victoria comes to the throne
1869   Work is completed on the Suez Canal
1881   Work begins on the Panama Canal
1894   Queen Victoria opens the Manchester Ship Canal
1914   The Panama Canal is completed.
1932   Eleven companies merge to form the Grand Union Canal
1947   A transport act brings all canals except the Bridgewater and Manchester Ship Canal under national control

New Words

Aqueduct	A bridge to carry water
Bargee	Man in charge of a barge
Berth	Sleeping quarters on a boat
Blast out	To blow up rocks using explosives
Bow	The front of the boat
Colliery	Coal mine
Commodity	Goods
Containers	Very large cases in which goods are packed to make their transport easier
Detour	A round about way
Dispatch	Haste
Feat	A praiseworthy act
Freight	Cargo
Intermediate	In between
Isthmus	A narrow neck of land connecting two larger parts
Laden	Loaded
Moor	Tie up a boat
Navigation	Directing the course of a boat or vessel
Nomadic	Wandering
Packet boat	Passenger boat
Patronage	Support
Plies	Goes to and fro
Punt	To move a boat by pushing a pole

	against the bottom of a river or canal
Stern	The back of a boat
Tariff	The rate of the toll tax
Tarpaulin	Waterproof cloth or canvas covering
Toll	A tax of a few pence paid for the use of roads and canals
Uniformity	Consistency or sameness
Weir	Dam across a river to raise level of water above it

More Books

de Mare, E. *Your Book of Waterways* (Faber & Faber, 1965). The story of roads of water from river navigation to the inland canals.

Murphy, J. S. *How they were Built, Canals* (Oxford University Press, 1961). The work of the navvies and engineers who built the canals.

Rolt, L. T. C. *Look at Canals* (Hamish Hamilton, 1962). A well written account of the great canal age.

Ross, A. *Canals in Britain* (Blackwells, 1962). A simple little book on canal travel and cruising today.

Wickson, R. *Britain's Inland Waterways* (Methuen, 1968). A history and geography of Britain's canals. The book gives information about boats and boatmen.

Index

Picture Credits